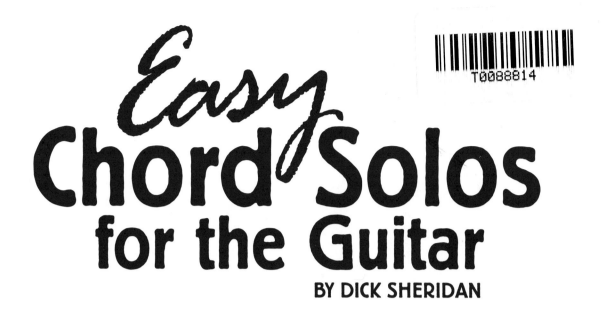

Easy Chord Solos for the Guitar

BY DICK SHERIDAN

To access audio visit:
www.halleonard.com/mylibrary

"Enter Code"
5042-1167-5403-8070

ISBN 978-1-57424-401-4
SAN 683-8022

Cover photo by Maureen Devey Jones

Copyright © 2021 CENTERSTREAM Publishing
P.O. Box 17878 - Anaheim Hills, CA 92817

www.centerstream-usa.com | centerstrm@aol.com | 714-779-9390

CONTENTS
25 Original Songs for the Guitar

FINGER LAKES SKETCHES

An Introduction

The following pages contain a collection of songs that you'll find relatively easy to play, some are simplicity itself, others a bit more challenging, but all will provide a lasting source of fun, interest and enjoyment.

PATTERNS

The songs are drawn from finger-picking patterns and chords -- a pattern being a repeated sequence of fingers of the right hand. Usually the same pattern is held throughout the song but variations can occur. For example, several different patterns may occur within the same song. Single notes not in a pattern may be introduced along with embellishment techniques like slides, hammer-ons, pull-offs and pinches (playing two notes together). A chord can be strummed instead of extracting its individual notes from a pattern.

CHORDS

The chords used for the following solos can be in ordinary form, inverted or altered. Chord diagrams serve to show their shape. Most of the chords are familiar and not difficult to play. Small changes to basic chords may occur but when they do they are easily managed. On rare occasions a "finger twister" might appear but that is unusual and fundamental shapes are the norm. In their basic form these chords can also be used for accompanying the song by another instrument.

TABLATURE

Tablature is an easy way of writing music for fretted string instruments and is used exclusively in this book rather than standard notation. TAB, as it is also called, simply shows what string is to be played and whether that string is to be played open or on what fret. Admittedly, tablature can be challenging at first for some players but with patience, practice and perseverance success will come. Audio tracks are included to further assist in interpreting the tablature and guiding the player as to the correct rhythm and tempo.

Although some of these pieces were written as learning songs for students, like many classical "études" (the French word for "studies") they are more than just that and are simply enjoyable to play.

As with the piece *Accompaniment To An Unwritten Song* found in this collection, some songs may indeed sound like accompaniments. But such songs can stand by themselves on their own merit. This is certainly true of J.S. Bach's *Prelude No.1 in C Major,* a chordal composition in its own right and subsequently used as the basis for Gounod's *Ave Maria.*

It is fair to call the following songs "miniatures." Most are short, some lasting only a few measures. Hopefully you'll agree that good things can come in small packages.

With the variety of fingering patterns and the broad diversity of chords and songs that lie ahead, there'll be no lack of choices to pick from. There's musical adventure in store and much rewarding discovery for all levels of players.

~*~

EXAMPLES OF PICKING PATTERNS

Let's take a look at some of the finger-picking patterns used in this book and the songs in which they are predominantly used. Time signatures used are 2/4, 3/4, 4/4 and 6/8.

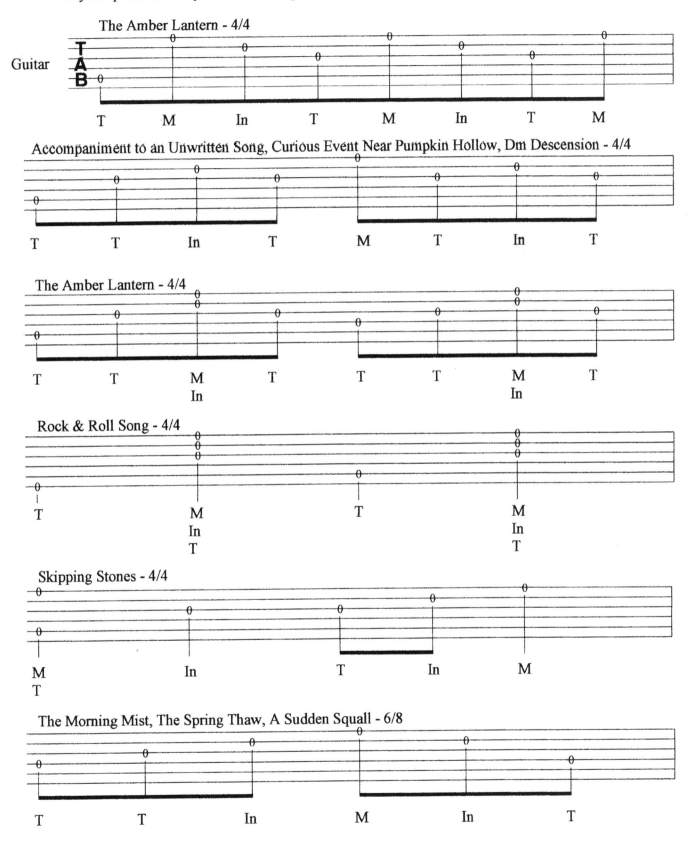

EXAMPLES OF PICKING PATTERNS

T=thumb, In=index (pointing) finger, M=middle finger

Contrary Motion, The Old Farmhouse, Pat's Song, Requiem, Ripples - 3/4

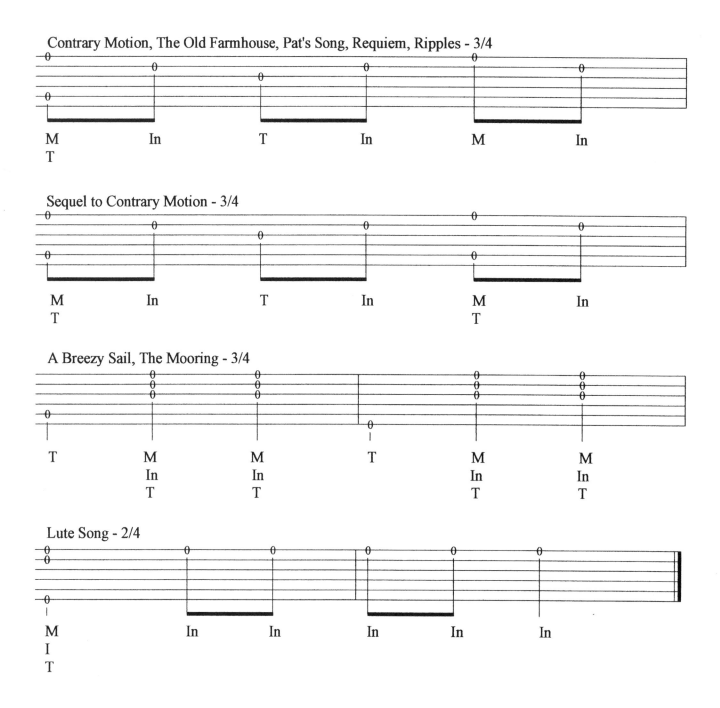

Sequel to Contrary Motion - 3/4

A Breezy Sail, The Mooring - 3/4

Lute Song - 2/4

The following songs have mixed or irregular patterns: Christmas Etude, The Colt, Lunar Stomp, The Regatta, and Whistle Britches.   However, the choice of which fingers to use is the same as with all the other songs - the thumb plays strings 6,5, and 4 - the index finger plays the 2nd string - and the middle finger (sometimes the index finger) plays the 1st string.

ACCOMPANIMENT TO AN UNWRITTEN SONG

Dick Sheridan

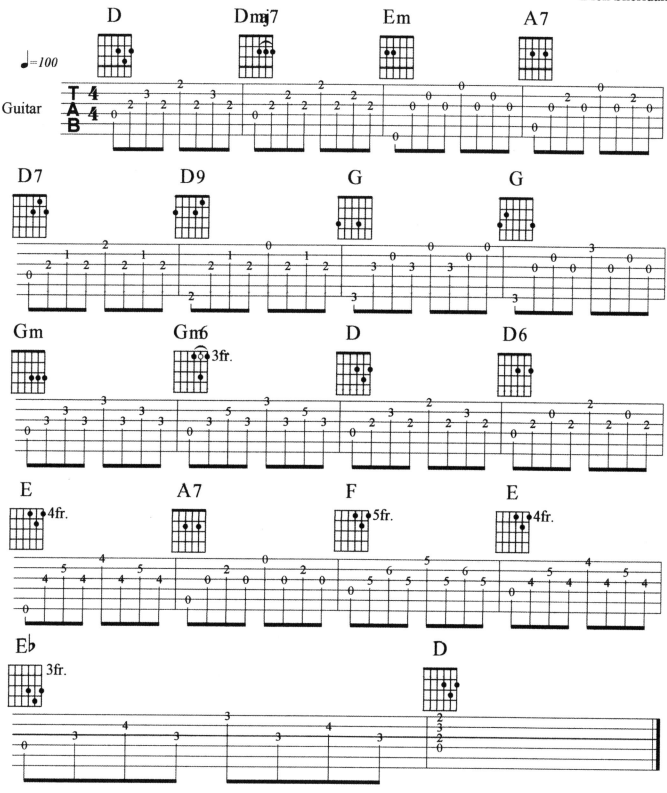

THE AMBER LANTERN
A Spanish Courtyard At Dusk

Dick Sheridan

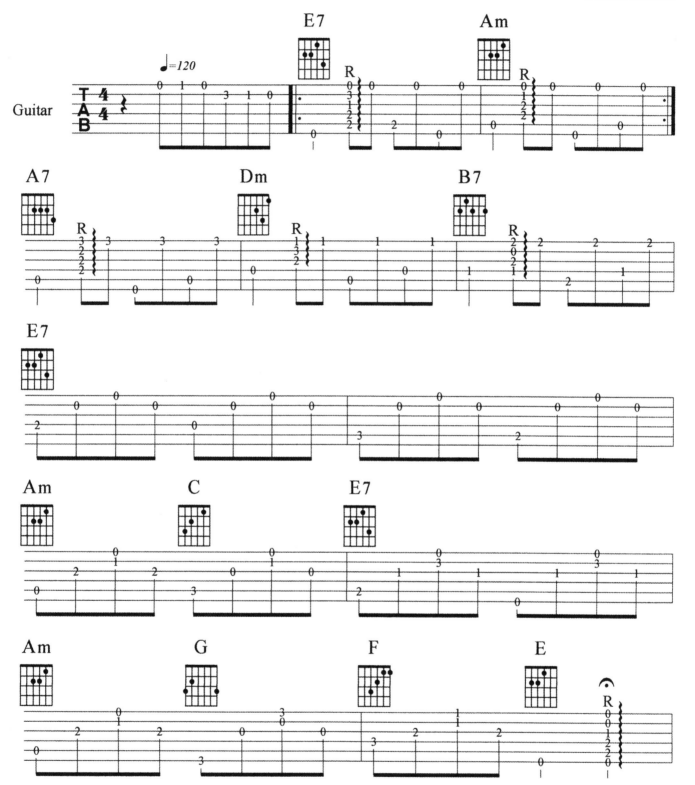

THE AMBER LANTERN

The RASQUEADO is a right-hand strumming technque typically associated with flamenco guitar music. The fingers are flaired out consecutively one after another in a rapid fan-like motion starting with the little finger and followed in succesion by the ring, middle and index fingers. It will be indicated by a vertical wavy line and the letter R.

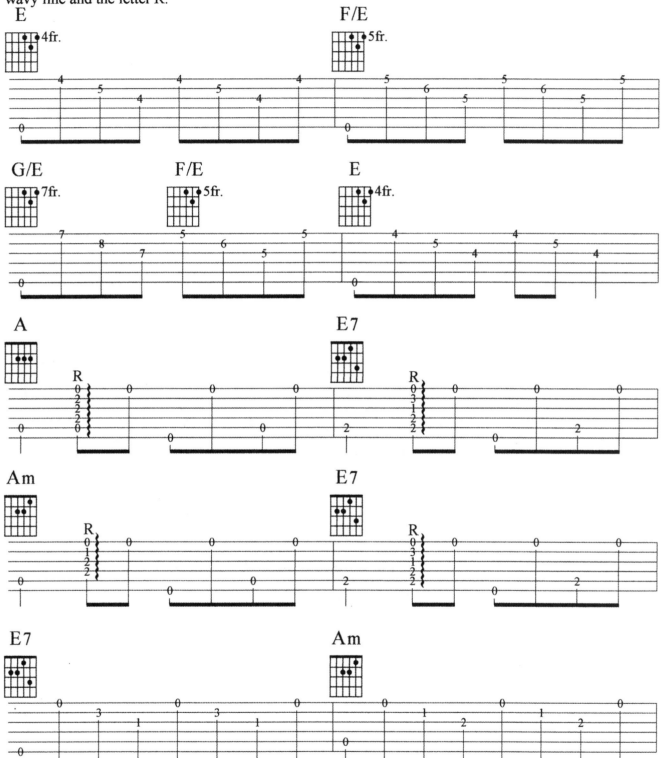

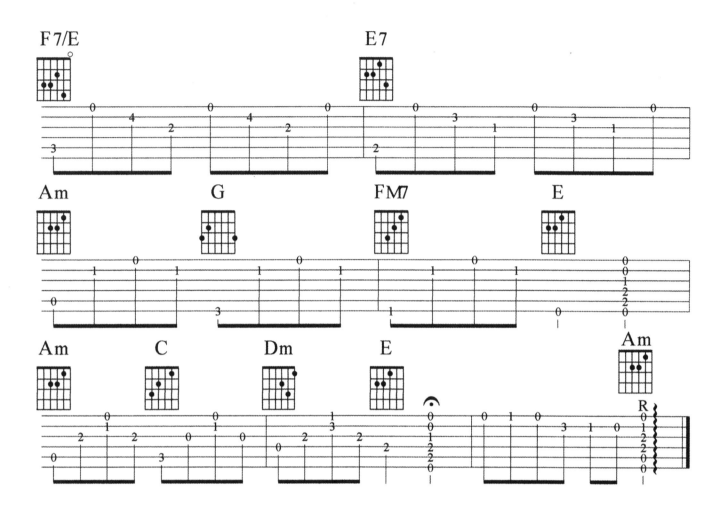

BOOM TOWN
A Little Mexican Restaurant

Dick Sheridan

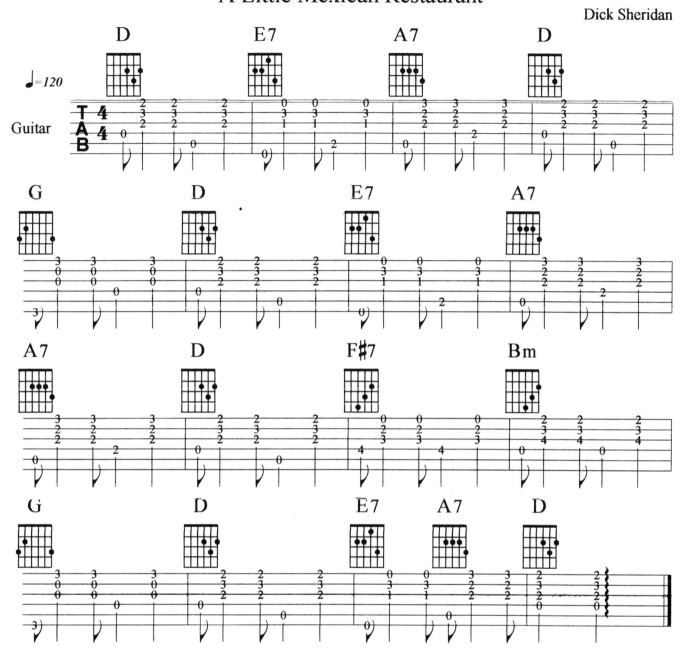

Going out to a restaurant was a rare treat for me as a child. Once when my mother was out of town my father took my sister and me to a little Mexican bistro called Boom Town in nearby Flushing on Long Island. Red and white checkered tablecloth, subdued lighting with candles mounted on green Cianti wine bottles wrapped in straw. Although the menu fare was surely Mexican -- tacos, chile, enchiladas and guacamole -- our children's meal was a special concession, a fiesta of spaghetti and meatballs. So long ago, but so unforgettable, and the memory lingers on. Olé!

CHRISTMAS ETUDE

Dick Sheridan

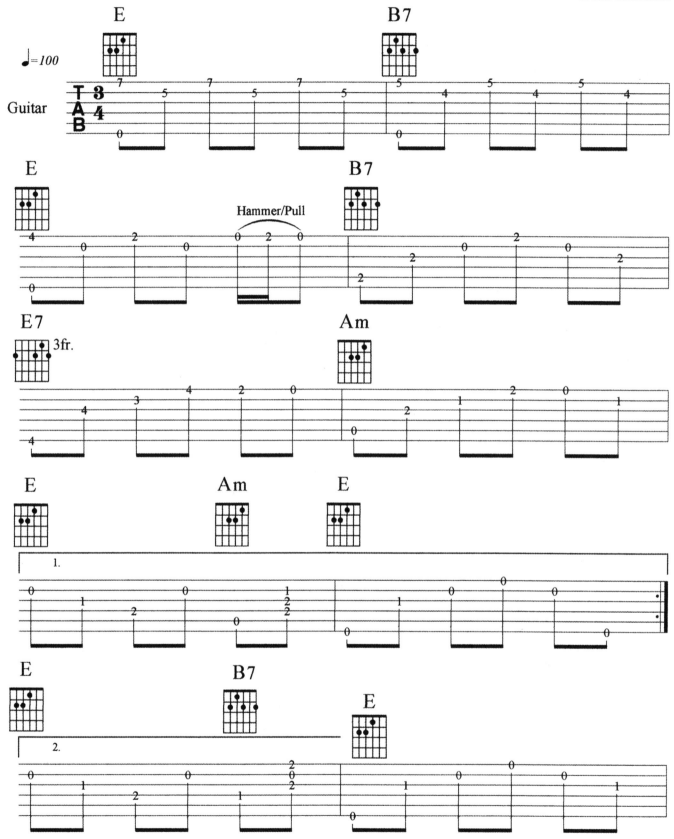

CHRISTMAS ETUDE

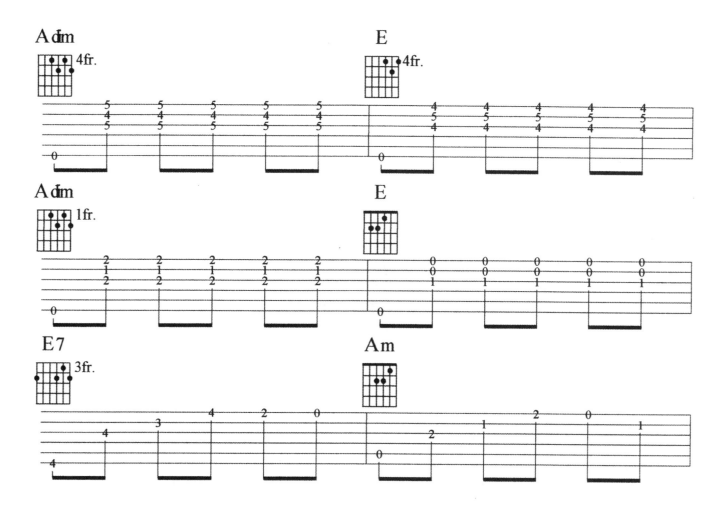

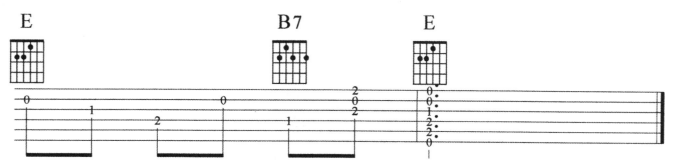

THE COLT

Dick Sheridan

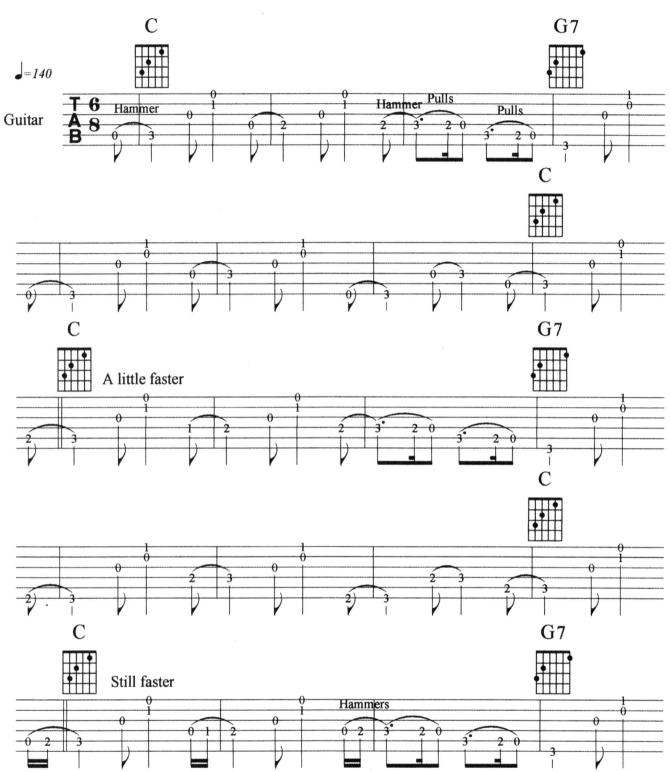

THE COLT

Imagine a frisky colt galloping round and round in the pasture, leaping, prancing and rearing until exhausted, out of breath, and panting. You can imitate the sound of panting by grasping the wound 6th string (low E) between thumb and 1st finger of the right hand, then sliding fingers back and forth over the sound hole.

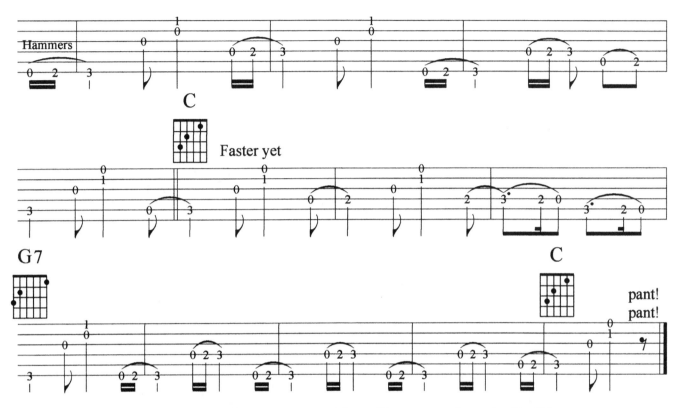

The curved line called "a slur" can represent either a "hammer-on" or a "pull off."

A hammer-on is made by playing an open string or fret and without picking the string again bringing a finger down hard on a higher fret, thus sounding two notes with only one picking motion. Sometimes two or more frets can be sounded with only one picking motion.

A pull-off is made by fingering a fret and without playing the string again snapping the finger to a lower fret or open string. Like the hammer-on this sounds two notes with only one picking motion. In *The Colt* multiple pull-offs occur.

In measures #3 and #4 (and in similar subsquent measures) there's a series of a hammer-on and pull-offs. The sequence is as follows:

> A hammer-on from 2 to 3, then a pull-off from 3 to 2,
> another pull-off from 2 to the open string.
> Without picking the string again there's a hammer-on from open to 3,
> followed by a pull-off from 3 to 2 and another pull-off from 2 to open.

That makes a sounding of six pull-off notes with the left hand and only a single picking motion.

CONTRARY MOTION

Phil Ryan & Dick Sheridan

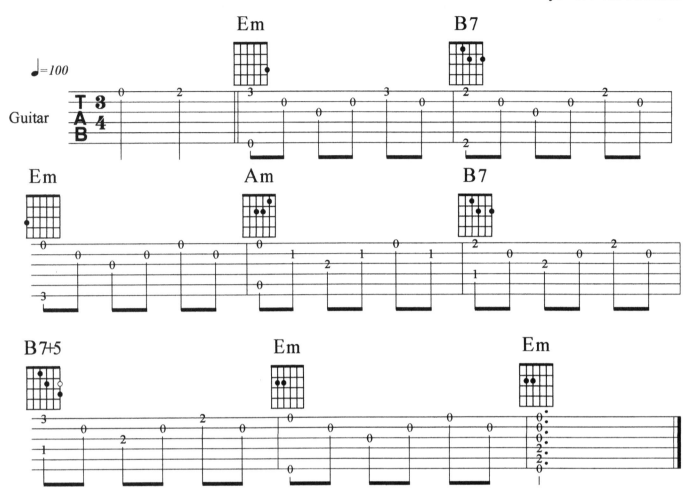

A college classmate stopped by my dormitory room one day and spotted my Yamaha folk guitar propped up in a corner. He was a trombone player, not a guitaist, and a member of our campus Dixieland jazz band. In some capacity he had spent summers with the celebrated Trapp Family Singers at their lodge in Stowe, Vermont. Picking up my guitar he started playing the low 6th string and 1st string together, ascending on the low string and descending on the high string. Inadvertently he had discoverd contrary motion. With the addition of a few chords and a picking pattern thus was born this little piece.

The open circle in the B7+5 chord is what I call a "phantom dot." It indicates the placement of a finger but whose sound is overridden by another note on the same string.

THE CURIOUS EVENT
NEAR PUMPKIN HOLLOW

Dick Sheridan

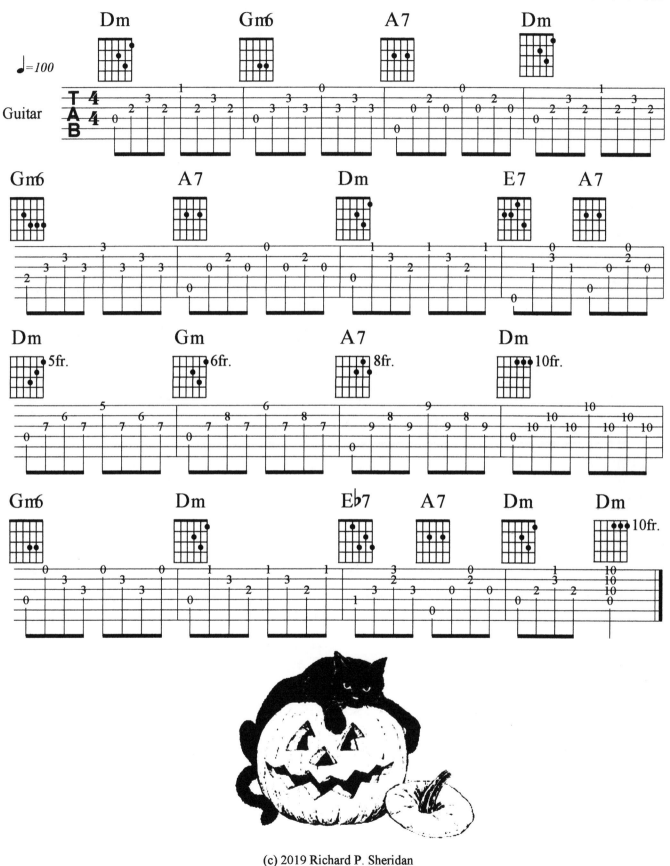

D MINOR DESCENSION

Dick Sheridan

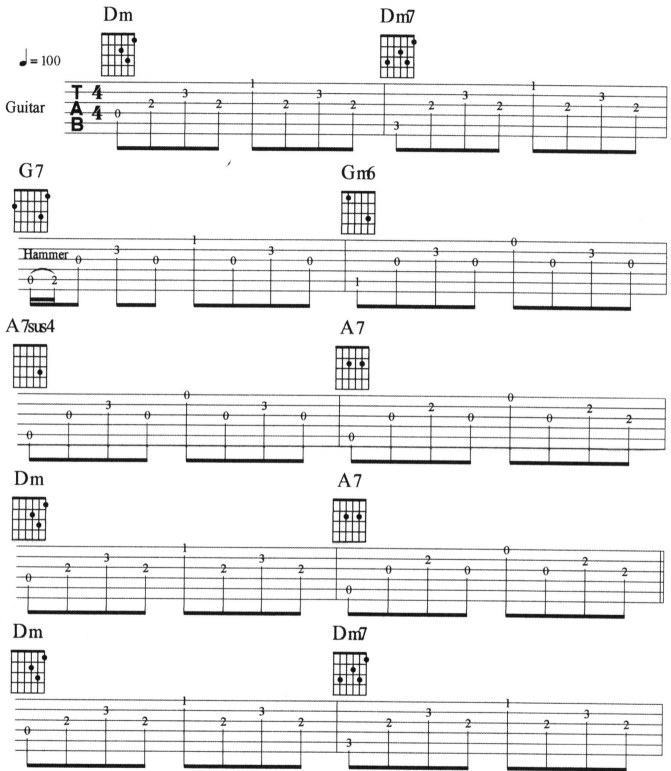

18

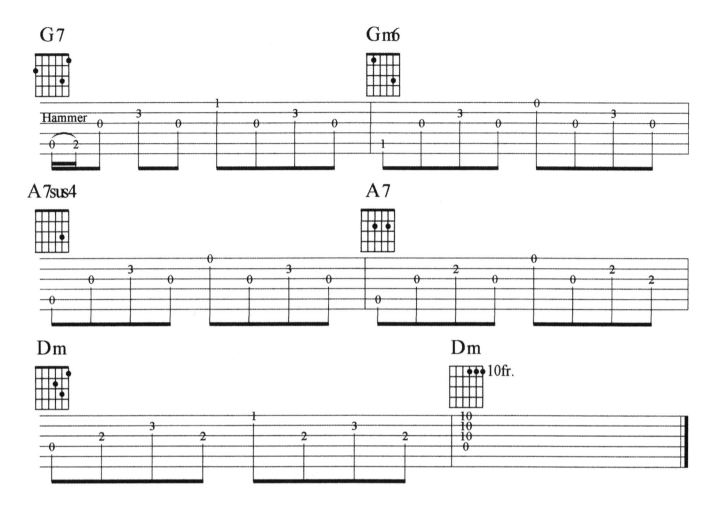

FASTER THAN WITCHES

Dick Sheridan

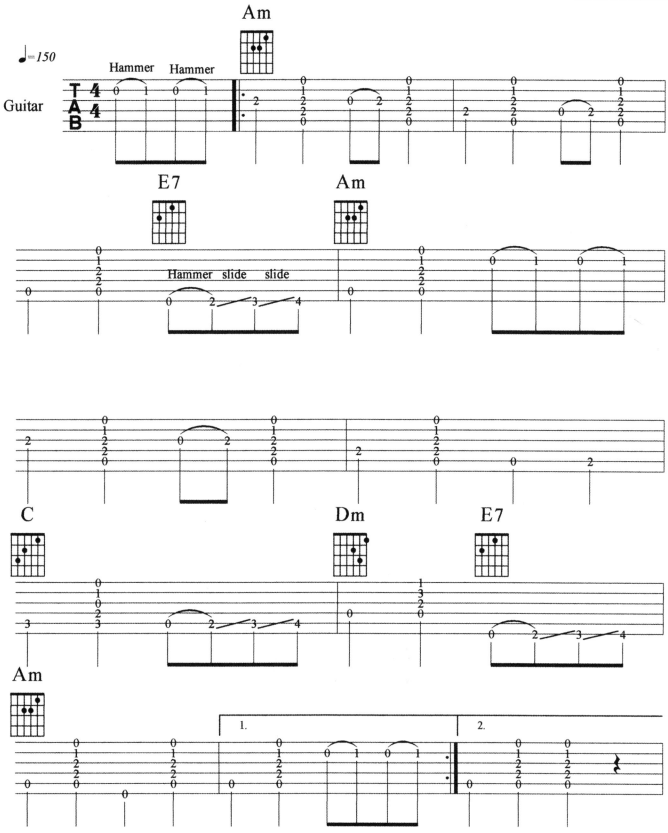

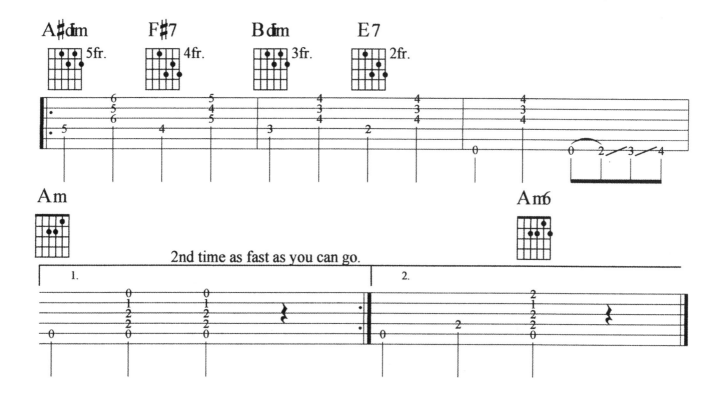

2nd time as fast as you can go.

Song title from a poem *The Railway Carriage* in Robert Louis Stevenson's *A Child's Garden Of Verses.*
"Faster than fairies, faster than witches,
Bridges and houses, hedges and ditches ..."

LUNAR STOMP

Dick Sheridan

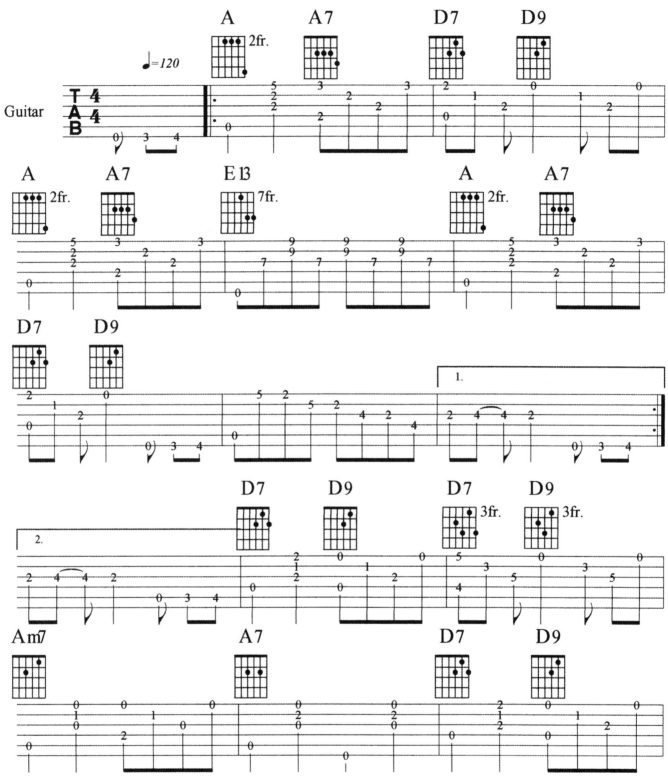

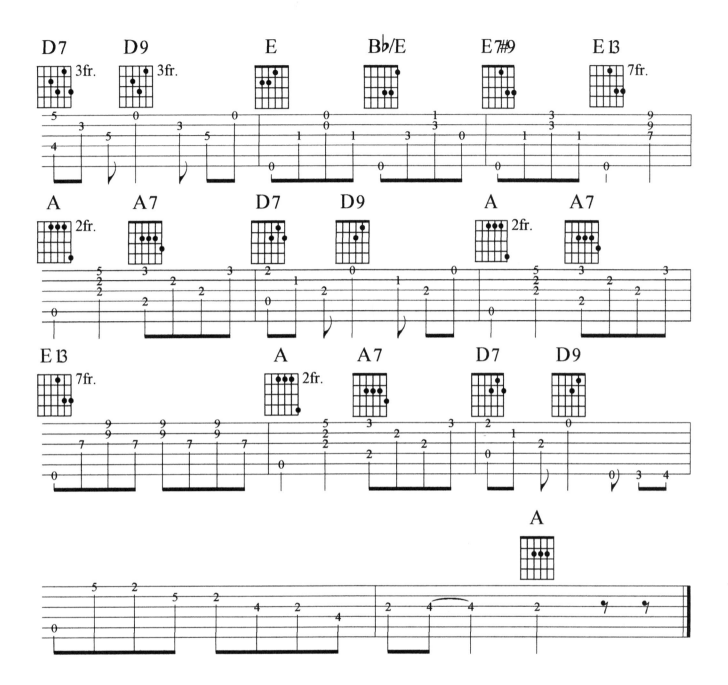

Author's note: *Lunar Stomp* evolved from the *Rock & Roll Song* included elsewhere in this book. I was slumped in a chair playing my guitar the night of July 20, 1969 while watching the landing of the Apollo lunar module and the first walk on the moon by astronauts Neil Armstrong and Buzz Aldrin.

LUTE STUDY

Dick Sheridan

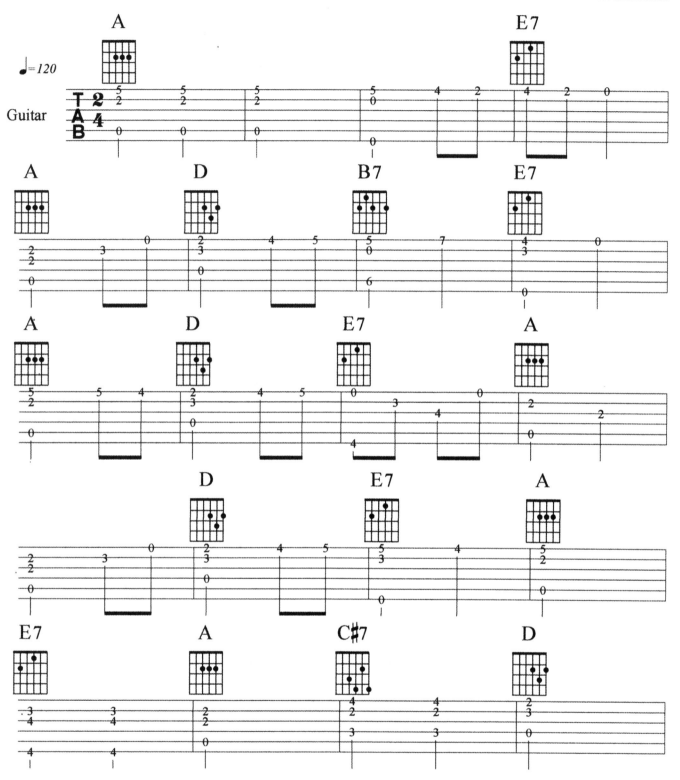

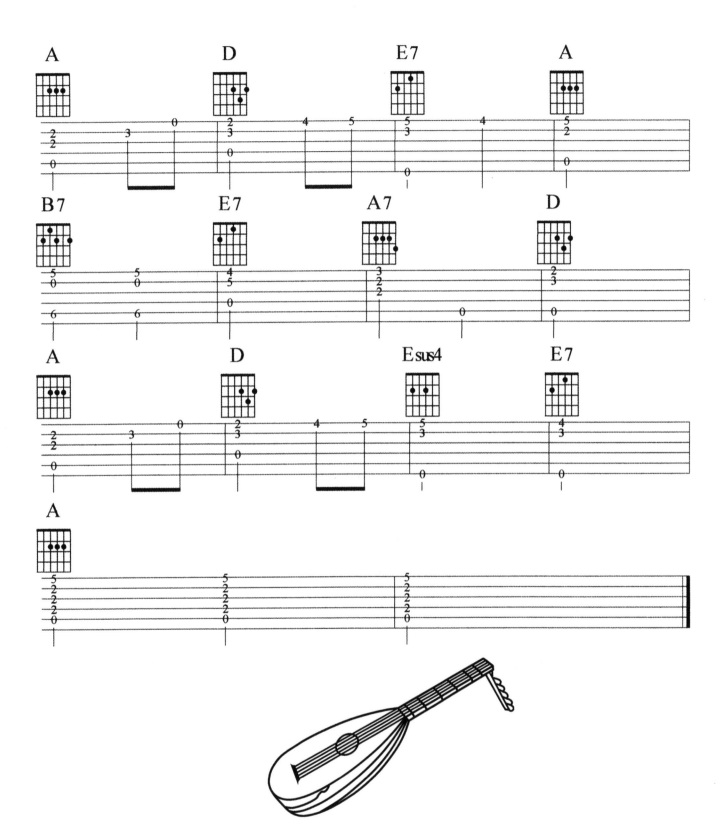

PAT'S SONG

Dick Sheridan

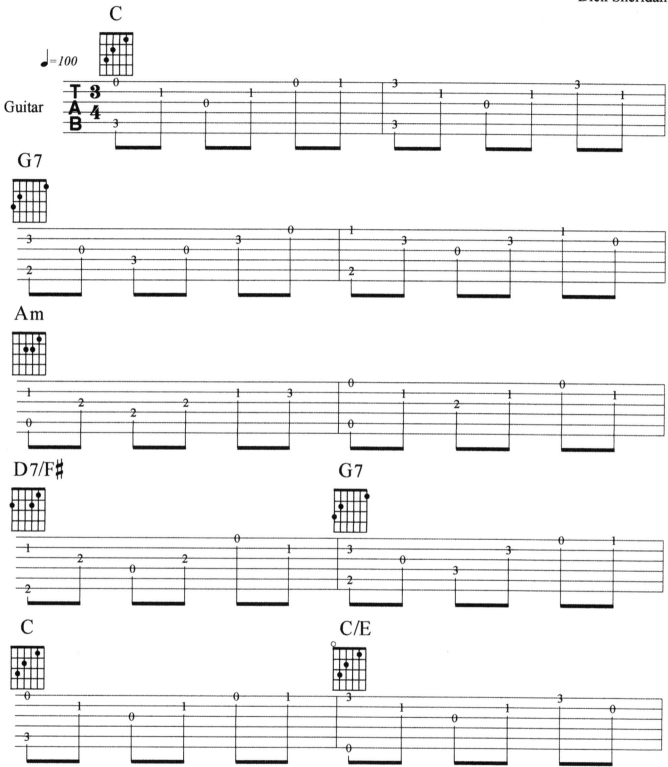

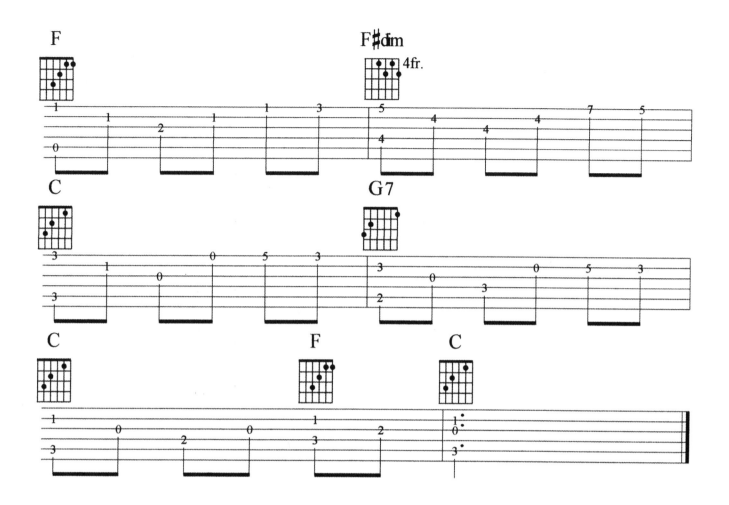

REQUIEM

Dick Sheridan

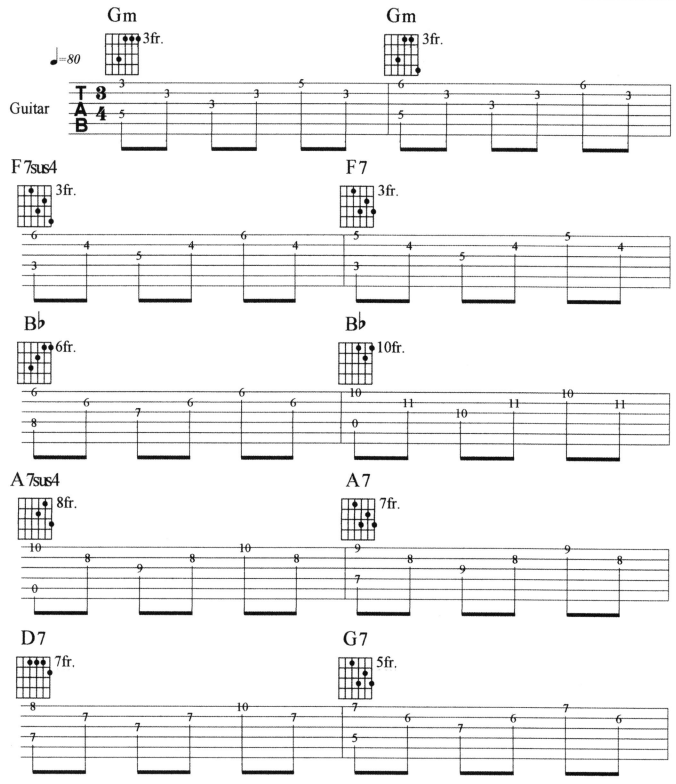

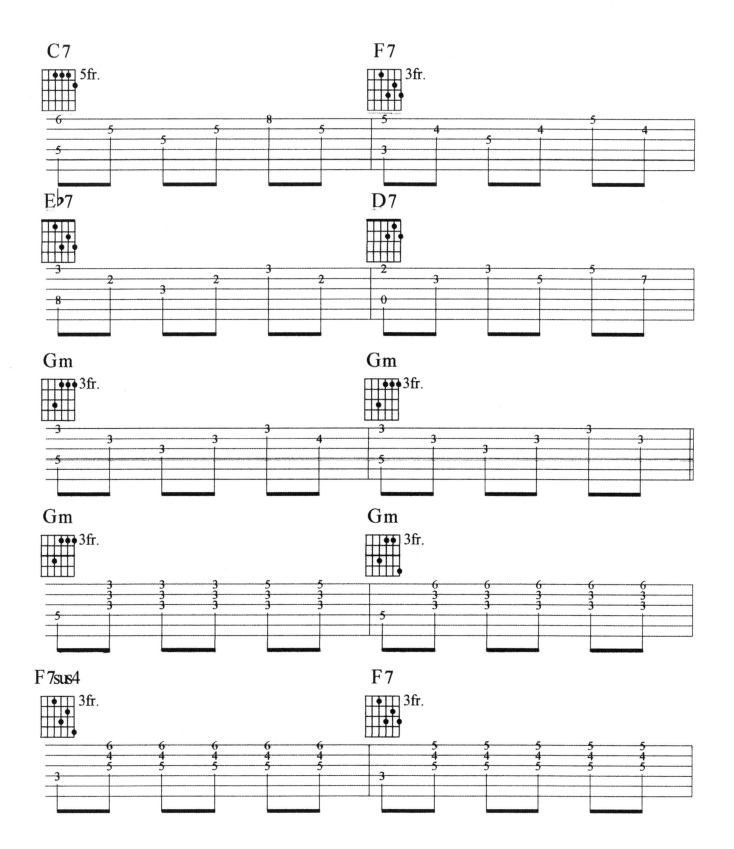

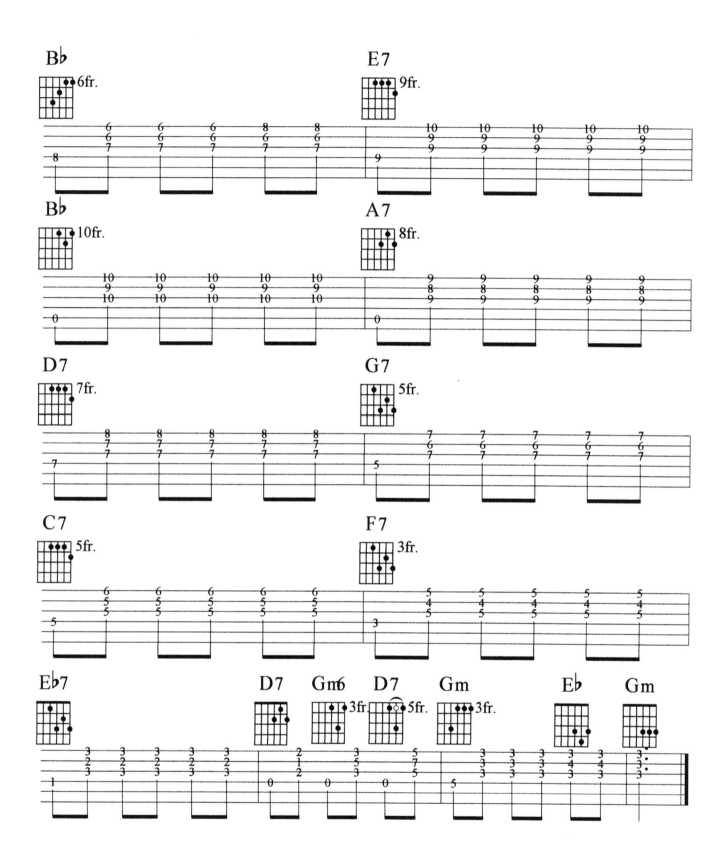

RIPPLES

Dick Sheridan

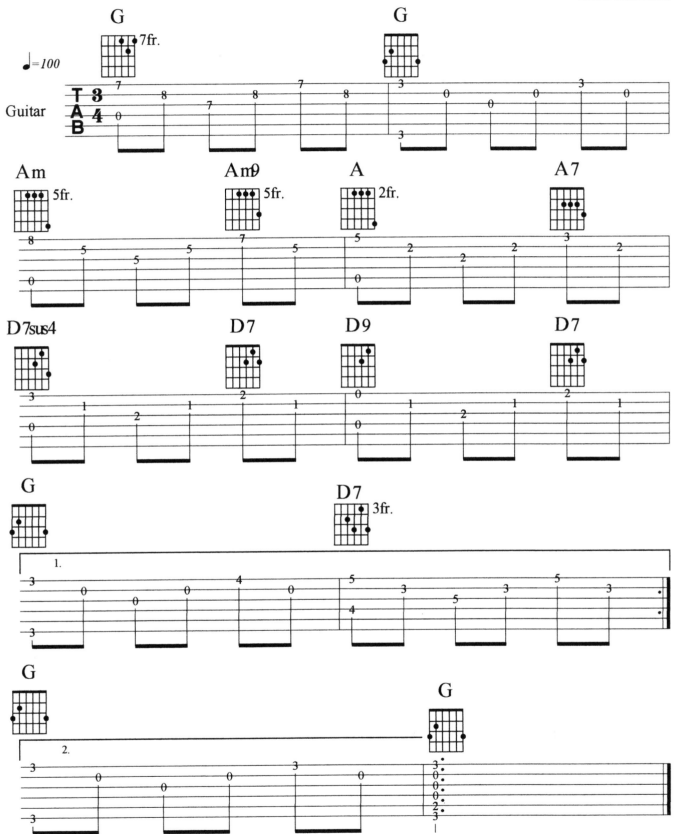

ROCK & ROLL SONG

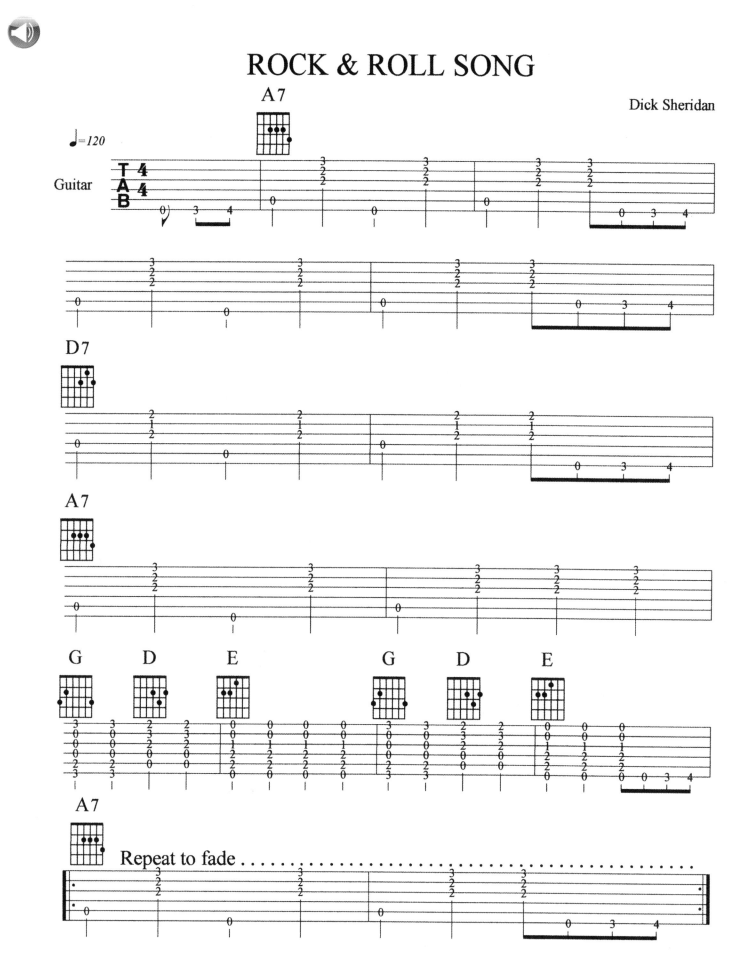

SEQUEL TO CONTRARY MOTION

Dick Sheridan

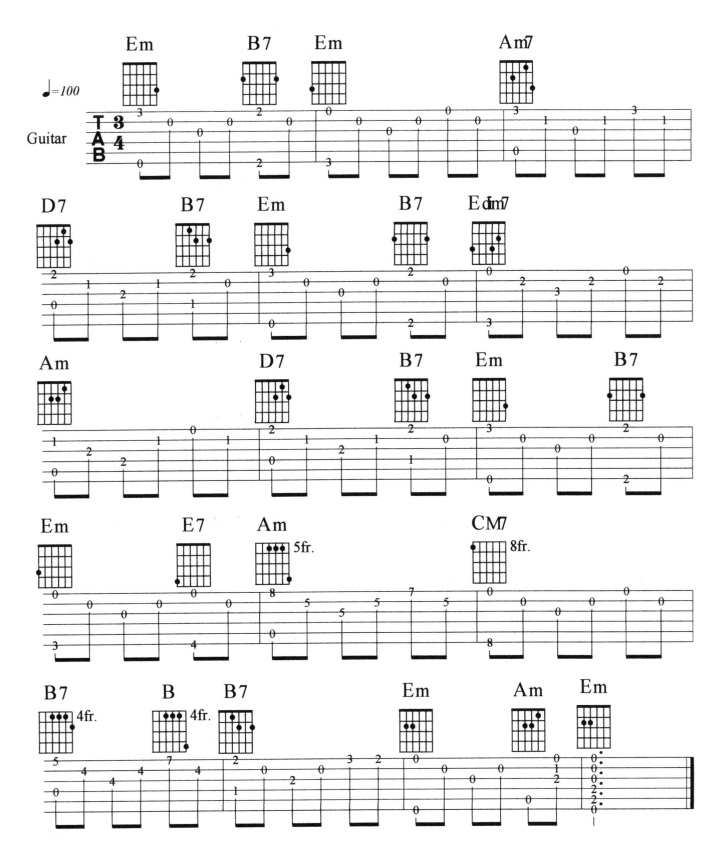

WHISTLE BRITCHES

Dick Sheridan

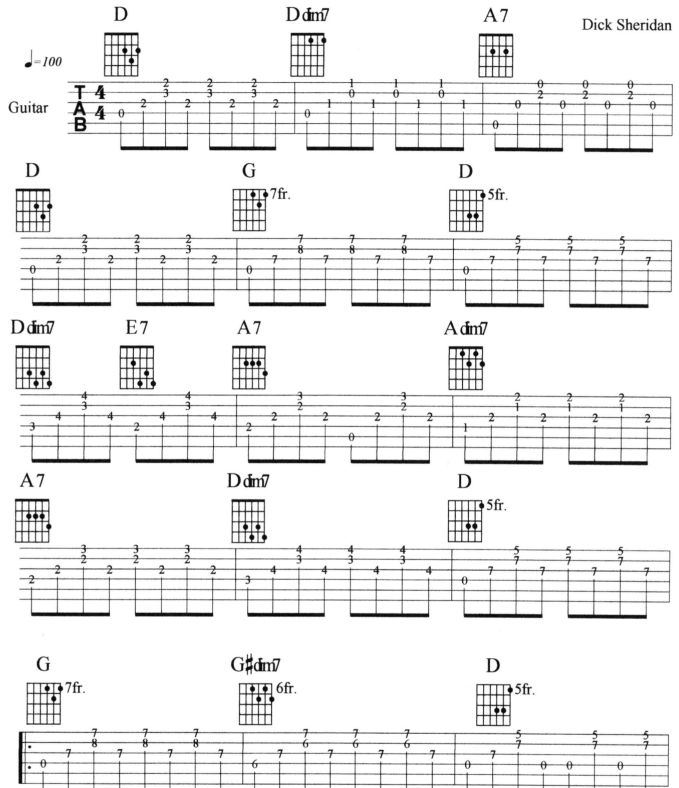

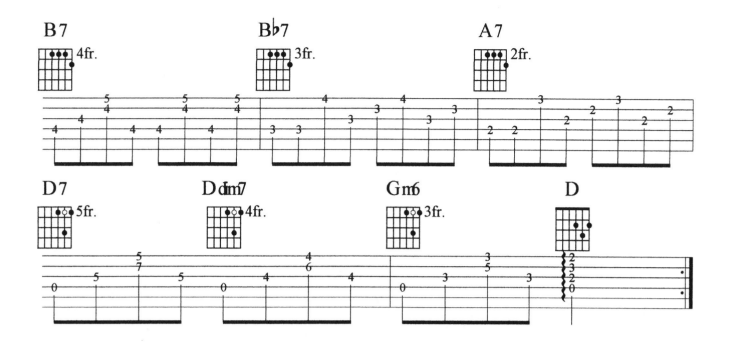

If you've ever worn corduroy pants then you'll know the sound as one leg rubs against the other. Hence the title of this little piece.

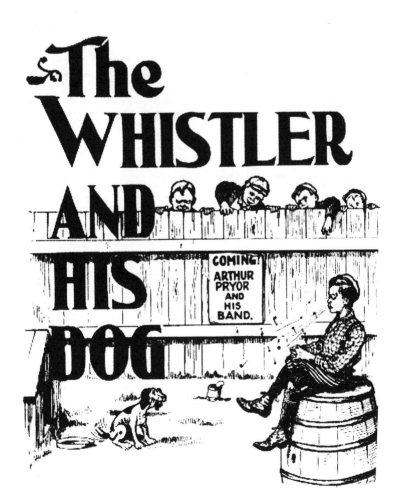

THE SPRING THAW

Dick Sheridan

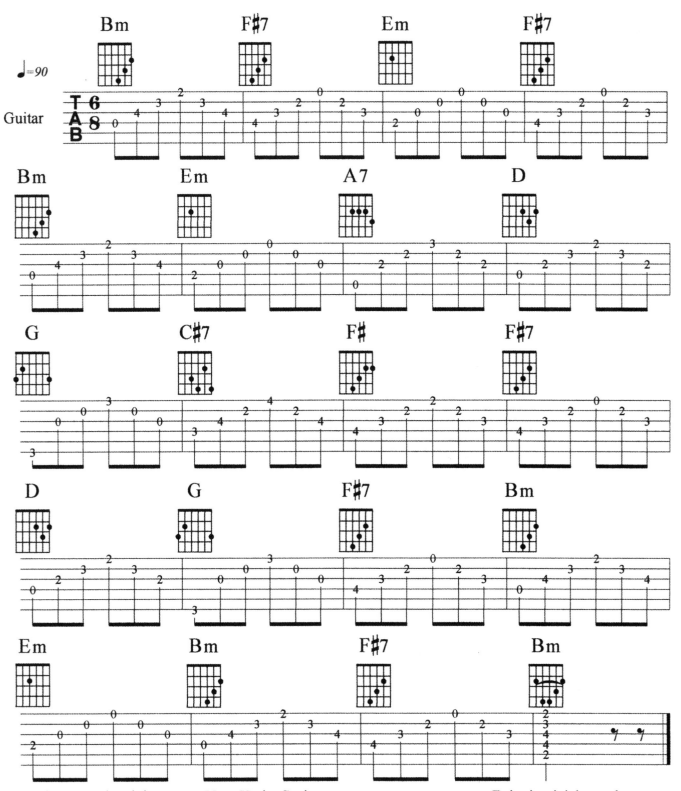

Winters are harsh in upstate New York. Spring can never come too soon. Dripping icicles and melting snow are a welcome prelude to warmer days, returning birds, and the eruption of nature.

Finger Lakes Sketches
A Word from the Author

To many inland dwellers, the Finger Lakes located in upstate New York are a touch of the sea, remarkably simulating the appearance, behavior, and temperament of the ocean and Great Lakes beyond. In time, if you live in the area long enough, it is inevitable that you become acutely sensitive to these lakes, alert to their every mood and expression, especially to the changes wrought in them by weather and the play of the seasons.

Having lived in upstate New York for over 60 years, I find the Finger Lakes constant companions. Several of these lakes I know better than others, namely those closest to Syracuse. One lake, Skaneateles, visible from the north windows of my remodeled schoolhouse, I see daily; the others are not far off and frequently seen under virtually every condition imposed by man or nature.

According to legend, the name of these fresh water lakes come from the Native Americans living in the region who envisioned the lakes as the imprint of the hand of the Great Spirit. As these impression were filled with water the lakes were formed.

It is surprising to many that there are 11 Finger Lakes, not five. The six largest ones are often incorrectly thought of as being the only Finger Lakes; they include Skaneateles, Owasco, Cayuga, Seneca, Canandaigua, and Keuka. It is these lakes that have inspired the musical sketches that follow, along with Otisco Lake which is one of the five smaller lakes referred to as the Little Finger Lakes -- Conesus, Hemlock, Canadice, and Honeoye.

It is Otisco Lake, in fact, that inspired this small collection of guitar solos. The composition of that name was born late one summer afternoon while visiting the lake side cottage of a friend. I was practicing a new style of "finger picking" and watching the setting sun create patterns of diamonds and multi-color sparkles in the shimmering water.

Once having submitted to the first indulgence of attempting to capture in music the impression of one lake and its vicinity, the other lakes began clamoring for expression, and before I realized it, a collection of reflections was in the process of creation.

Both the nearby and outlying lakes return to mind as I had originally seen them, and it is these reminiscences that I have tried to interpret for the guitar. The companion pieces in this collection are not unrelated to the lake sketches. For they too attempt in their own fashion to portray as harmonically as possible certain places, things, and events unique in my experience and memory of the Finger Lakes area.

These Finger Lakes Sketches, together with their companion compositions, will I hope combine to form a musical folio of sufficient attractiveness to challenge the interests and talents of guitarists at varying levels of proficiency. It is further hoped that they will also appeal to the imagination and in some degree the aesthetics and enjoyment of those who may hear them.

CANANDAIGUA LAKE
A Breezy Sail

Dick Sheridan

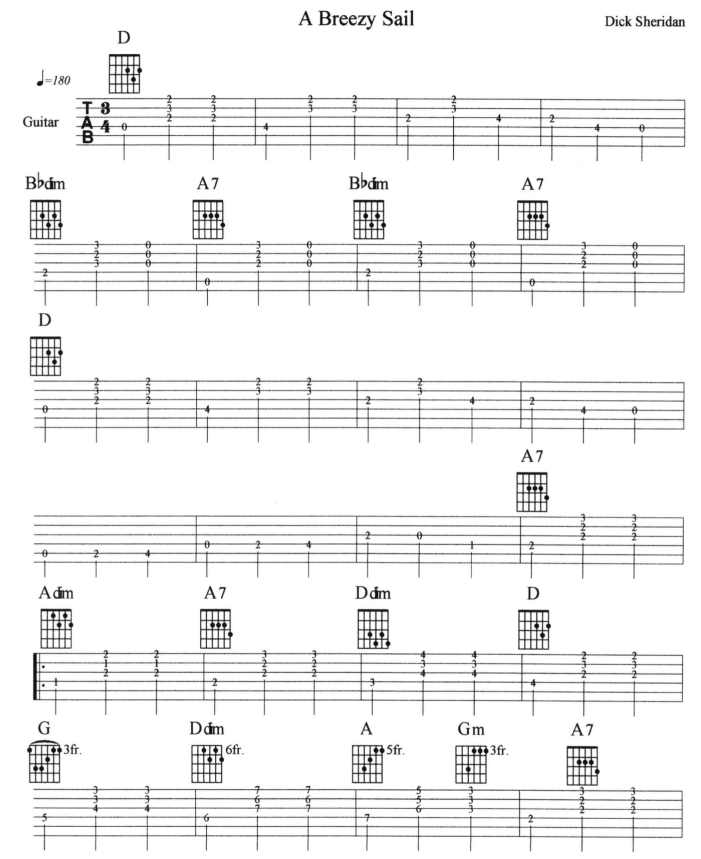

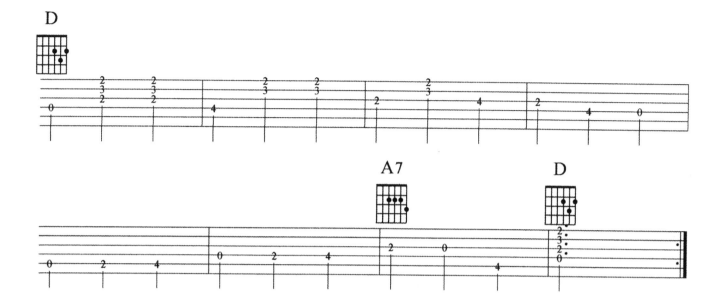

CAYUGA LAKE
The Mooring

Dick Sheridan

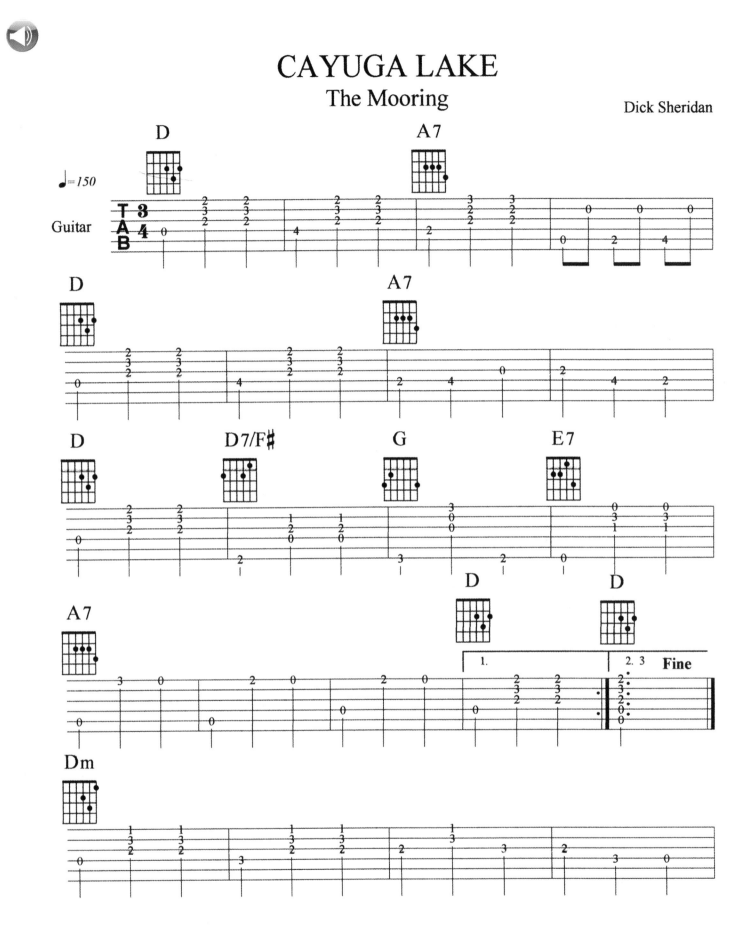

THE MOORING

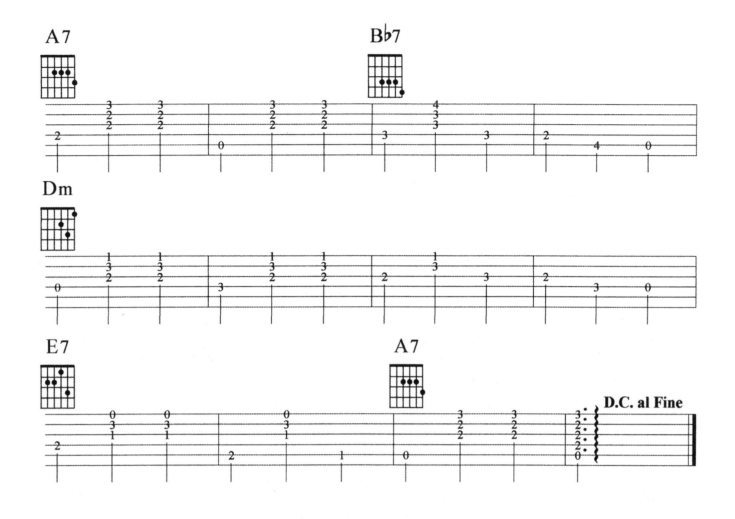

KEUKA LAKE
The Morning Mist

Dick Sheridan

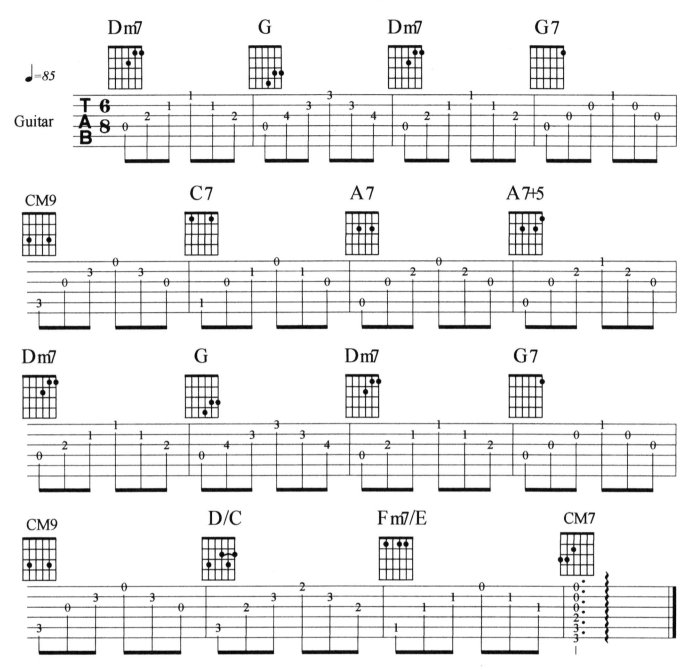

After the heat of a long summer day, the chill of the following morning spreads a foggy mist over the warm waters of Keuka Lake. Here and there steam clouds rise to meet the early sun, and the promise is for another beautiful day in upstate central New York. Surrounded by sloping hills and vinyards, the Y-shaped lake was once known as Crooked Lake or in the language of the Seneca Indians "lake with an elbow."

OTISCO LAKE
Skipping Stones

Dick Sheridan

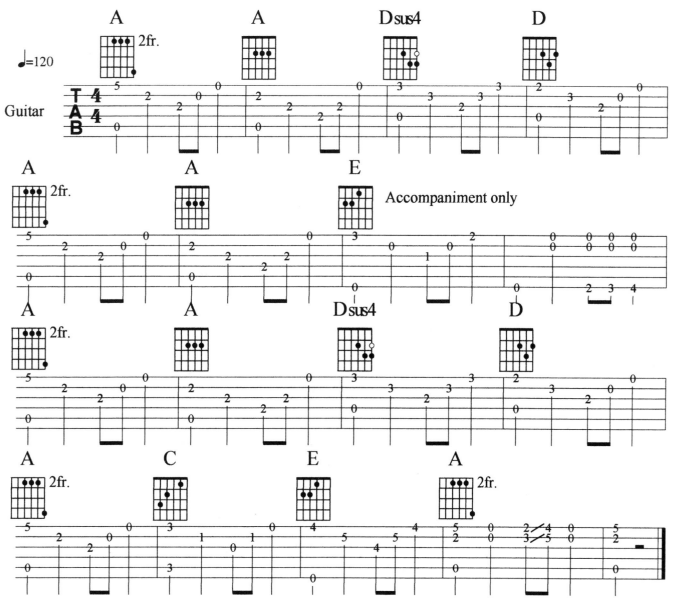

Otisco Lake is one of the small Finger Lakes south of the city of Syracuse, NY. It is the easternmost of New York's 11 Finger Lakes. Five and a half miles long and 3/4 miles at its widest point, its waters flow eventually to Lake Ontario, one of North America's five Great Lakes. Lakes like Otisco bring childhood memories of standing on the shore and throwing stones to see how many times they could bounce on the water before sinking. Competitions developed to see whose stone could bounce the most.

OWASCO LAKE
The Old Farmhouse

Dick Sheridan

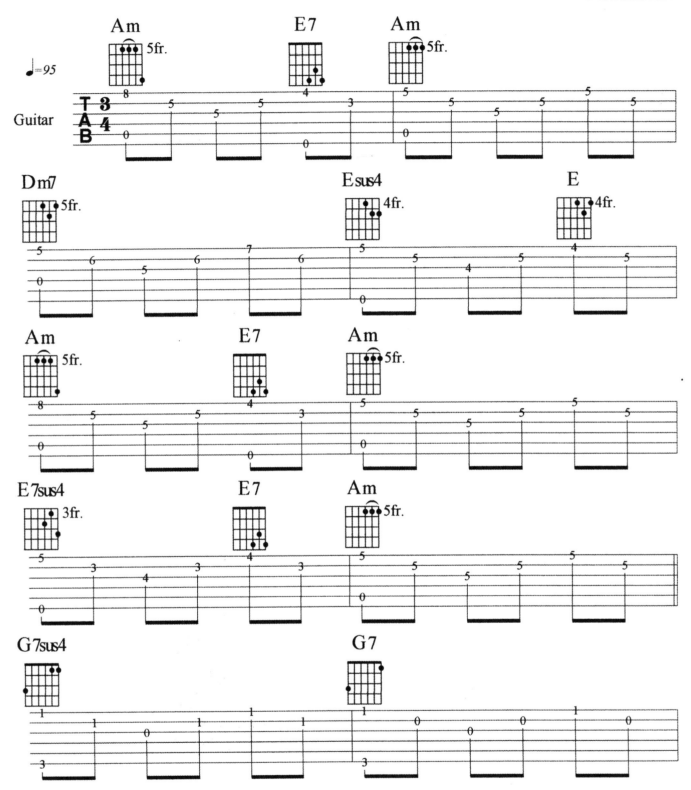

THE OLD FARMHOUSE

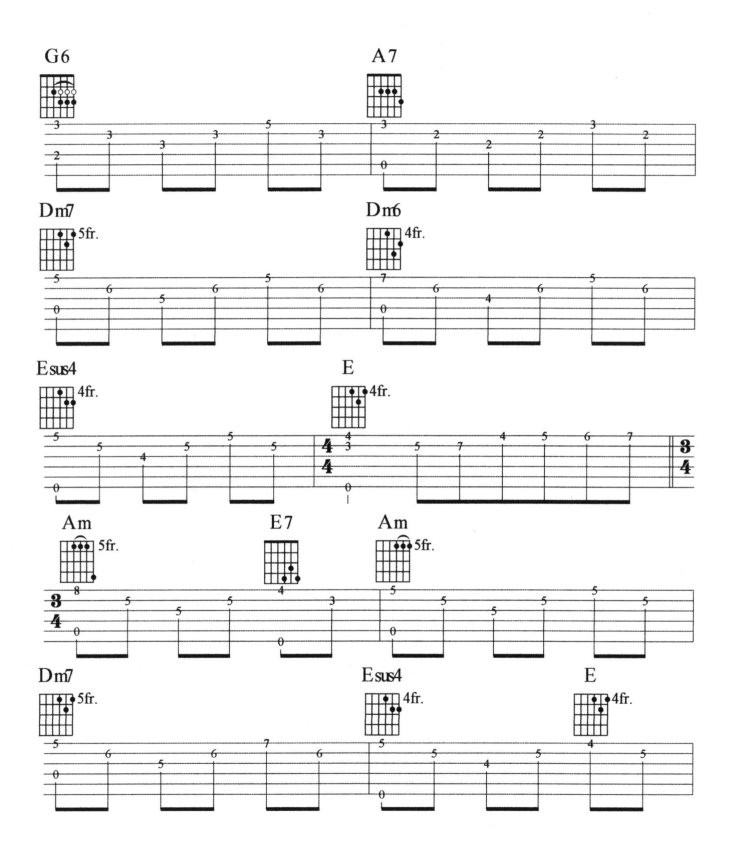

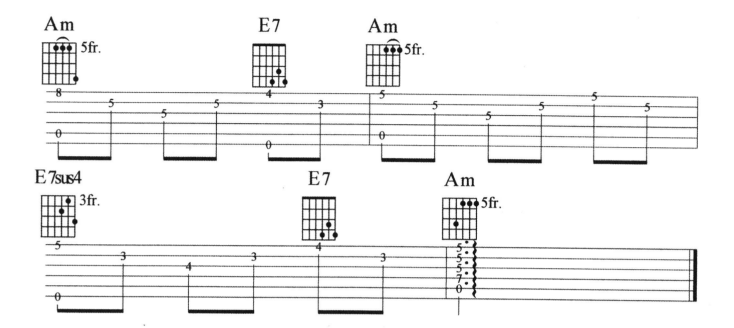

For a related poetry reading, see Joyce Kilmer's *The House With Nobody In It.*

SENECA LAKE
A Sudden Squall

Dick Sheridan

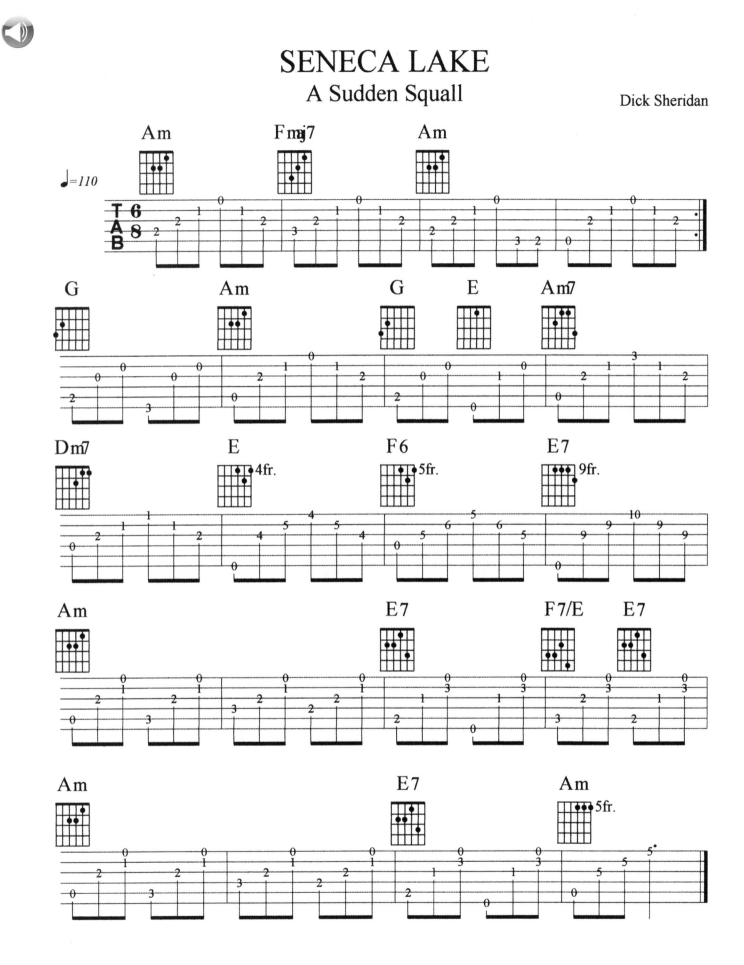

SKANEATELES LAKE
The Regatta

Dick Sheridan

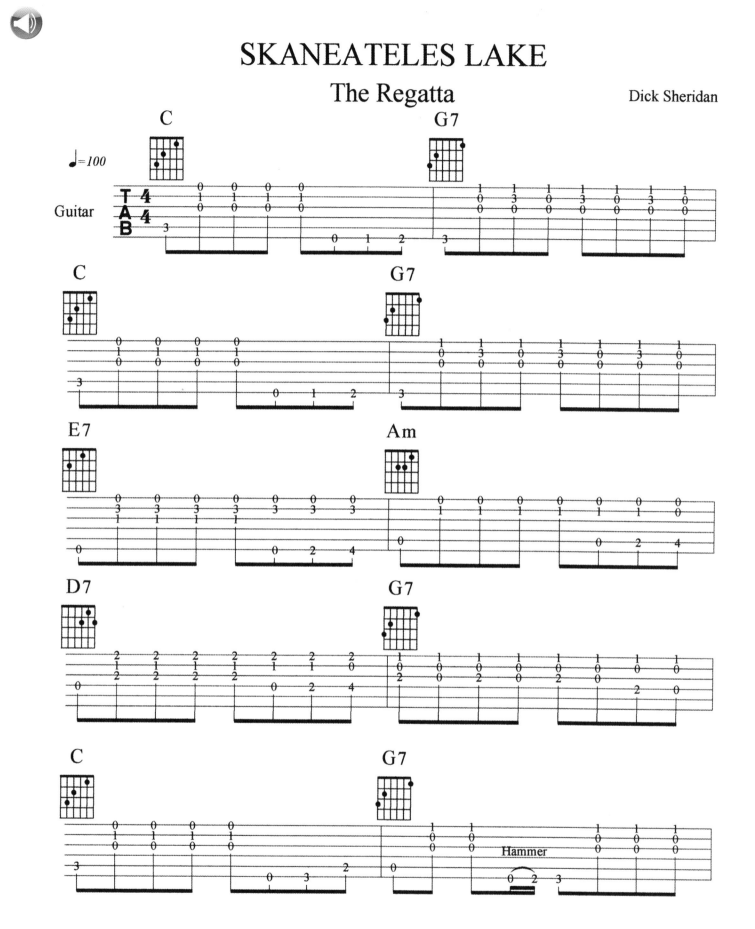

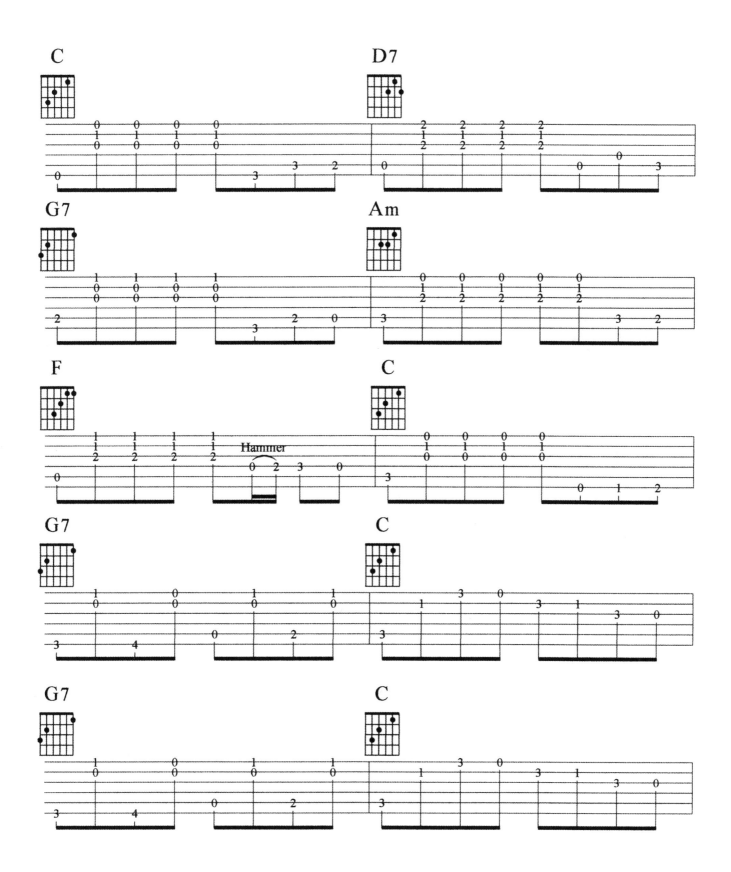

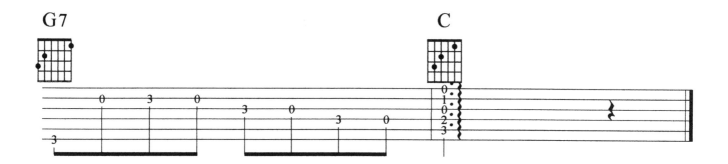

The name "Skaneateles" is a tough one to pronounce.
Broken down into syllables it's SKAN-ee-AT-less or simply SKINNY ATLAS. The 16-mile lake
is known as the Eastern Gateway to the five main Finger Lakes. Its pure water supplies the city of
Syracuse and its rural shores are surrounded by farms.summer cottages and year-round homes. As
the glaciers that formed the lake moved south, they left gentle rolling landscape to the north then dug
deeply into the ground leaving steep hills, towering cliffs and rocky embankments. Noted by one
visitor, the south end reminded him of the fiords of his native homeland in Norway. The village of
Skaneateles at the north end of the lake is home to interesting shops and eateries like the popular
Sherwood Inn and Krebbs restaurant, both in operation for over 100 years. The town library houses
an excellent gallery of paintings by local artist John D. Barrow (1824-1906). The lake is well-known
for its regatta of sailboats as well as for its annual Antique and Classic Boat Show. Come the holiday
season and the village transforms to a Dickens Christmas complete with traditional mid-1800 costumes,
horse-drawn wagons, roasting chestnuts, and strolling carollers.

More Great Books from Dick Sheridan...

More Great Guitar Books from Centerstream...

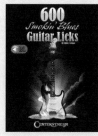
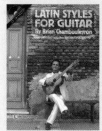

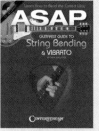